THE CRISIS

THOMAS PAINE

THE CRISIS

penguin books

PENGUIN BOOKS
Published by the Penguin Group
Penguin Books USA Inc., 375 Hudson Street,
New York, New York 10014, U.S.A.
Penguin Books Ltd, 27 Wrights Lane,
London W8 5TZ, England
Penguin Books Australia Ltd, Ringwood,
Victoria, Australia
Penguin Books Canada Ltd, 10 Alcorn Avenue,
Toronto, Ontario, Canada M4V 3B2
Penguin Books (N.Z.) Ltd, 182–190 Wairau Road,
Auckland 10, New Zealand

Penguin Books Ltd, Registered Offices:
Harmondsworth, Middlesex, England

Published in Penguin Books 1995

ISBN 0 14 60.0101 X

Printed in the United States of America

THE CRISIS

Number I

December 23, 1776

These are the times that try men's souls: The summer soldier and the sunshine patriot will, in this crisis, shrink from the service of his country; but he that stands it NOW, deserves the love and thanks of man and woman. Tyranny, like hell, is not easily conquered; yet we have this consolation with us, that the harder the conflict, the more glorious the triumph. What we obtain too cheap, we esteem too lightly: 'Tis dearness only that gives every thing its value. Heaven knows how to put a proper price upon its goods; and it would be strange indeed, if so celestial an article as FREEDOM should not be highly rated. Britain, with an army to enforce her tyranny, has declared that she has a right (*not only to* TAX) but *"to* BIND *us in* ALL CASES WHATSOEVER," and if being *bound in that manner,* is not slavery, then is there not such

I

a thing as slavery upon earth. Even the expression is impious, for so unlimited a power can belong only to GOD.

Whether the independence of the continent was declared too soon, or delayed too long, I will not now enter into as an argument; my own simple opinion is, that had it been eight months earlier, it would have been much better. We did not make a proper use of last winter, neither could we, while we were in a dependent state. However, the fault, if it were one, was all our own; we have none to blame but ourselves. But no great deal is lost yet; all that Howe has been doing for this month past is rather a ravage than a conquest, which the spirit of the Jerseys a year ago would have quickly repulsed, and which time and a little resolution will soon recover.

I have as little superstition in me as any man living, but my secret opinion has ever been, and still is, that God Almighty will not give up a people to military destruction, or leave them unsupportedly to perish, who had so earnestly and so repeatedly sought to avoid the calamities of war, by every decent method which wisdom could invent. Neither have I so much of the infidel in me, as to suppose that HE has relinquished the government of the world, and given us up to the care of devils; and as I do not, I cannot see on what grounds the king of Britain can look up to Heaven for help against us: A common murderer, a highwayman, or a house-breaker has as good a pretence as he.

'Tis surprising to see how rapidly a panic will sometimes run through a country. All nations and ages have been subject to them: Britain has trembled like an ague at the report of a French fleet of flat bottomed boats; and in the fourteenth century the whole English army, after ravaging the kingdom of France, was driven back like men petrified with fear; and this brave exploit was performed by a few broken forces collected and headed by a woman, Joan of Arc. Would, that Heaven might inspire some Jersey maid to spirit up her countrymen, and save her fair fellow sufferers from ravage and ravishment! Yet panics, in some cases, have their uses, they produce as much good as hurt. Their duration is always short; the mind soon grows through them, and acquires a firmer habit than before. But their peculiar advantage is, that they are the touchstones of sincerity and hypocrisy, and bring things and men to light, which might otherwise have lain for ever undiscovered. In fact, they have the same effect on secret traitors, which an imaginary apparition would have

3

upon a private murderer. They sift out the hidden thoughts of man, and hold them up in public to the world. Many a disguised tory has lately shewn his head, that shall penitentially solemnize with curses the day on which Howe arrived upon the Delaware.

As I was with the troops at Fort-Lee, and marched with them to the edge of Pennsylvania, I am well acquainted with many circumstances, which those, who lived at a distance, know but little or nothing of. Our situation there was exceedingly cramped, the place being on a narrow neck of land between the North-River and the Hackensack. Our force was inconsiderable, being not one fourth so great as Howe could bring against us. We had no army at hand to have relieved the garrison, had we shut ourselves up and stood on the defence. Our ammunition, light artillery, and the best part of our stores, had been removed upon the apprehension that Howe would endeavor to penetrate the Jerseys, in which case Fort-Lee could be of no use to us; for it must occur to every thinking man, whether in the army or not, that these kind of field forts are only for temporary purposes, and last in use no longer than the enemy directs his force against the particular object, which such forts are raised to defend.

Such was our situation and condition at Fort-Lee on the morning of the 20th of November, when an officer arrived with information that the enemy with 200 boats had landed about seven or eight miles above: Major General Greene, who commanded the garrison, immediately ordered them under arms, and sent express to his Excellency General Washington at the town of Hackensack, distant by the way of the ferry six miles. Our first object was to secure the bridge over the Hackensack, which laid up the river between the enemy and us, about six miles from us, and three from them. General Washington arrived in about three quarters of an hour, and marched at the head of the troops towards the bridge, which place I expected we should have a brush for; however they did not choose to dispute it with us, and the greatest part of our troops went over the bridge, the rest over the ferry, except some which passed at a mill on a small creek, between the bridge and the ferry, and made their way through some marshy grounds up to the town of Hackensack, and there passed the river. We brought off as much baggage as the waggons could contain, the rest was lost. The simple object was to bring off the garrison, and to march them on till they could be strengthened by the Jersey or Pennsylvania militia, so as to be enabled to make a stand. We staid four days at Newark, collected in our out-posts with some of the Jersey militia, and marched out twice to meet the enemy on information of their being advancing, though our numbers were greatly inferior to theirs. Howe, in my little opinion, committed a great error in generalship in not throwing a body of forces off from Staten-Island through Amboy, by which means he might have seized all our stores at Brunswick, and intercepted our march into Pennsylvania: But if we believe the power of hell to be limited, we must likewise believe that their agents are under some providential controul.

I shall not now attempt to give all the particulars of our retreat to the Delaware; suffice it for the present to say, that both officers and men, though greatly harassed and fatigued, frequently without rest, covering, or provision, the inevitable consequences of a long retreat bore it with a manly and a marital spirit. All their wishes were one, which was, that the country would turn out and help them to drive the enemy back. Voltaire has remarked that King William never appeared to full advantage but in difficulties and in action; the same remark may be made on General Washington, for the character fits him. There is a natural firmness in some minds which cannot be un-locked by trifles, but which, when unlocked, discovers a cabinet of fortitude; and I reckon it among those kind of public blessings, which we do not immediately see, that GOD hath blest him with uninterrupted health, and given him a mind that can even flourish upon care.

I shall conclude this paper with some miscellaneous remarks on the state of our affairs; and shall begin with asking the following question, Why is it that the enemy have left the New-England provinces, and made these middle ones the seat of war? The answer is easy: New-England is not infested with tories, and we are. I have been tender in raising the cry against these men, and used numberless arguments to shew them their danger, but it will not do to sacrifice a world to either their folly or their baseness. The period is now arrived, in which either they or we must change our sentiments, or one or both must fall. And what is a tory? Good GOD! what is he? I should not be afraid to go with an hundred whigs against a thousand tories, were they to attempt to get into arms. Every tory is a coward, for a servile, slavish, self-interested fear is the foundation of toryism; and a man under such influence, though he may be cruel, never can be brave.

But, before the line of irrecoverable separation be drawn between us, let us reason the matter together: Your conduct is an invitation to the enemy, yet not one in a thousand of you has heart enough to join him. Howe is as much deceived by you as the American cause is injured by you. He expects you will all take up arms, and flock to his standard with muskets on your shoulders. Your opinions are of no use to him, unless you support him personally, for 'tis soldiers, and not tories, that he wants.

I once felt all that kind of anger, which a man ought to feel, against the mean principles that are held by the tories: A noted one, who kept a tavern at Amboy, was standing at his door, with as pretty a child in his hand, about eight or nine years old, as most I ever saw, and after speaking his mind as freely as he thought was prudent, finished with his unfatherly expression, *"Well! give me peace in my day."* Not a man lives on the continent but fully believes that a separation must some time or other finally take place, and a generous parent should have said, *"If there must be trouble, let it be in my day that my child may have peace;"* and this single reflection, well applied, is sufficient to awaken every man to duty. Not a place upon earth might be so happy as America. Her situation is remote from all the wrangling world, and she has nothing to do but to trade with them. A man may easily distinguish in himself between temper and principle, and I am as confident, as I am that GOD governs the world, that America will never be happy till she gets clear of foreign dominion. Wars, without ceasing, will break out till that period arrives, and the continent must in the end be conqueror; for though the flame of liberty may sometimes cease to shine, the coal never can expire.

America did not, nor does not want force; but she wanted a proper application of that force. Wisdom is not the purchase of a day, and it is no wonder that we should err at first setting off. From an excess of tenderness, we were unwilling to raise an army, and trusted our cause to the temporary defence of a well-meaning militia. A summer's experience has now taught us better; yet with those troops, while they were collected, we were able to set bounds to the progress of the enemy, and, thank GOD! they are again assembling. I always considered a militia as the best troops in the world for a sudden exertion, but they will not do for a long campaign. Howe, it is possible, will make an attempt on this city, should he fail on this side of the Delaware, he is ruined; If he succeeds, our cause is not ruined. He stakes all on his side against a part on ours; admitting he succeeds, the consequence will be, that armies from both ends of the continent will march to assist their suffering friends in the middle states; for he cannot go every where, it is impossible. I consider Howe as the greatest enemy the tories have; he is bringing a war into their country, which, had it not been for him and partly for themselves, they had been clear of. Should he now be expelled, I wish with all the devotion of a Christian, that the names of whig and tory may never more be mentioned; but should the tories give him encouragement to come, or assistance if he come, I as sincerely wish that our next year's arms may expel them from the continent, and the congress appropriate their possessions to the relief of those who have suffered in well-doing. A single successful battle next year will settle the whole. America could carry on a two years war by the confiscation of the property of disaffected persons, and be made happy by their expulsion. Say not that this is revenge, call it rather the soft resentment of a suffering people, who, having no object in view but the GOOD of ALL, have staked their OWN ALL upon a seemingly doubtful event. Yet it is folly to argue against determined hardness; eloquence may strike the ear, and the language of sorrow draw forth the tear of compassion, but nothing can reach the heart that is steeled with prejudice.

Quitting this class of men, I turn with the warm ardor of a friend to those who have nobly stood, and are yet determined to stand the matter out: I call not upon a few, but upon all; not on THIS state or THAT state, but on EVERY state; up and help us; lay your shoulders to the wheel; better have too much force than too little, when so great an object is at stake. Let it be told to the future world, that in the depth of winter, when nothing but hope and virtue could survive, that the city and the country, alarmed at one common danger, came forth to meet and to repulse it. Say not, that thousands are gone, turn out your tens of thousands; throw not the burden of the day upon Providence, but *"shew your faith by your works,"* that God may bless you. It matters not where you live, or what rank of life you hold, the evil or the blessing will reach you all. The far and the near, the home counties and the back, the rich and the poor, will suffer or rejoice alike. The heart that feels not now, is dead: The blood of his children will curse his cowardice, who shrinks back at a time when a little might have saved the whole, and made *them* happy. I love the man that can smile in trouble, that can gather strength from distress, and grow brave by reflection. 'Tis the business of little minds to shrink; but he whose heart is firm, and whose conscience approves his conduct, will pursue his principles unto death. My own line of reasoning is to myself as strait and clear as a ray of light. Not all the treasures of the world, so far as I believe, could have induced me to support an offensive war, for I think it murder; but if a thief break into my house, burn and destroy my property, and kill or threaten to kill me, or those that are in it, and to *"bind me in all cases whatsoever,"* to his absolute will, am I to suffer it? What signifies it to me, whether he who does it, is a king or a common man; my countryman or not my countryman? whether it is done by an individual villain, or an army of them? If we reason to the root of things we shall find no difference; neither can any just case be assigned why we should punish in the one case and pardon in the other. Let them call me rebel, and welcome, I feel no concern from it; but I should suffer the misery of devils, were I to make a whore of my soul by swearing allegiance to one whose character is that of a sottish, stupid, stubborn, worthless, brutish man. I conceive likewise a horrid idea in receiving mercy from a being, who at the last day shall be shrieking to the rocks and mountains to cover him, and fleeing with terror from the orphan, the widow, and the slain of America.

There are cases which cannot be overdone by language, and this is one. There are persons too who see not the full extent of the evil which threatens them, they solace themselves with hopes that the enemy, if they succeed, will be merciful. It is the madness of folly to expect mercy from those who have refused to do justice; and even mercy, where conquest is the object, is only a trick of war: The cunning of the fox is as murderous as the violence of the wolf; and we ought to guard equally against both. Howe's first object is partly by threats and partly by promise, to terrify or seduce the people to deliver up their arms, and receive mercy. The ministry recommended the same plan to Gage, and this is what the tories call making their peace; *"a peace which passeth all understanding"* indeed! A peace which would be the immediate forerunner of a worse ruin than any we have yet thought of. Ye men of Pennsylvania, do reason upon these things! Were the back counties to give up their arms, they would fall an easy prey to the Indians, who are all alarmed: This perhaps is what some tories would not be sorry for. Were the home counties to deliver up their arms, they would be exposed to the resentment of the back counties, who would then have it in their power to chastise their defection at pleasure. And were any one state to give up its arms, THAT state must be garrisoned by all Howe's army of Britons and Hessians to preserve it from the anger of the rest. Mutual fear is a principal link in the chain of mutual love, and woe be to that state that breaks the compact. Howe is mercifully inviting you to barbarous destruction, and men must be either rogues or fools that will not see it. I dwell not upon the powers of imagination; I bring reason to your ears; and in language as plain as A, B, C, hold up truth to your eyes.

I thank GOD that I fear not. I see no real cause for fear. I know our situation well, and can see the way out of it. While our army was collected, Howe dared not risk a battle, and it is no credit to him that he decamped from the White Plains, and waited a mean opportunity to ravage the defenceless Jerseys; but it is great credit to us, that, with a handful of man, we sustained an orderly retreat for near an hundred miles, brought off our ammunition, all our field-pieces, the greatest part of our stores, and had four rivers to pass. None can say that our retreat was precipitate, for we were near three weeks in performing it, that the country might have time to come in. Twice we marched back to meet the enemy and remained out till dark. The sign of fear was not seen in our camp, and had not some of the cowardly and disaffected inhabitants spread false alarms through the country, the Jerseys had never been ravaged. Once more we are again collected and collecting; our new army at both ends of the continent is recruiting fast, and we shall be able to open the next campaign with sixty thousand men, well armed and cloathed. This is our situation, and who will may know it. By perseverance and fortitude we have the prospect of a glorious issue; by cowardice and submission, the sad choice of a variety of evils—a ravaged country—a depopulated city—habitations without safety, and slavery without hope—our homes turned into barracks and bawdy-houses for Hessians, and a future race to provide for whose fathers we shall doubt of. Look on this picture and weep over it! and if there yet remains one thoughtless wretch who believes it not, let him suffer it unlamented.

Number III (Selections)

Philadelphia, April 19, 1777

. . . after the coolest reflections on the matter, *this must* be allowed, that Britain was too jealous of America, to govern it justly; too ignorant of it, to govern it well; and too distant from it, to govern it at all. . . . All we want to know in America is simply this, who is for independence, and who is not? Those who are for it, will support it, and the remainder will undoubtedly see the reasonableness of their paying the charges; while those who oppose or seek to betray it, must expect the more rigid fate of the gaol and the gibbit. There is a bastard kind of generosity, which, by being extended to all men, is as fatal to society, on one hand, as the want of true generosity is on the other. A lax manner of administering justice, falsely termed moderation, has a tendency both to dispirit public virtue, and promote the growth of public evils.

The necessity of always fitting our internal police to the circumstances of the times we live in, is something so strikingly obvious that no sufficient objection can be made against it. The safety of all societies depend upon it; and where this point is not attended to, the consequences will either be a general languor or a tumult. The encouragement and protection of the good subjects of any state, and the suppression and punishment of bad ones, are the principal objects for which all authority is instituted, and the line in which it ought to operate. We have in this city a strange variety of men and characters, and the circumstances of the times require they should be publicly known; it is not the number of tories that hurt us, so much, as the not finding out who they are; men must now take one side or the other, and abide by the consequences. . . . If Britain cannot conquer us, it proves, that she is neither able to govern or protect us, and our particular situation now is such, that any connection with her would be unwisely exchanging a half defeated enemy for two powerful ones. Europe, by every appearance and information, is now on the eve, nay, on the morning twilight of a war, and any alliance with *George the third* brings *France* and *Spain* upon our backs; a separation from him attach them to our side; therefore, the only road to *peace*, *honor* and commerce is INDEPENDENCE.

Written this fourth year of the UNION, *which GOD preserve!*

Number IV (Selections)

Philadelphia, Sept. 12, 1777

Those who expect to reap the blessings of freedom, must, like men, undergo the fatigues of supporting it. The event of yesterday is one of those kind alarms which is just sufficient to rouse us to duty, without being of consequence enough to depress our fortitude. It is not a field of a few acres of ground, but a cause that we are defending, and whether we defeat the enemy in one battle, or by degrees, the consequence will be the same.

Look back at the events of last winter and the present year, there you will find that the enemy's successes have always contributed to reduce them. What they have gained in ground, they paid so dearly for in numbers, that their victories have in the end amounted to defeats. We have always been masters at the last push, and always shall while we do our duty. Howe has been once on the banks of the

Delaware, and from thence driven back with loss and disgrace; and why not be again driven from the Schuylkill? His condition and ours are very different. He has every body to fight, we have only his *one* army to cope with, and which wastes away at every engagement; we can not only reinforce, but can redouble our numbers; he is cut off from all supplies, and must sooner or later inevitably fall into our hands.

Shall a band of ten or twelve thousand robbers, who are this day fifteen hundred or two thousand men less in strength than they were yesterday, conquer America, or subdue even a single state? The thing cannot be, unless we sit down and suffer them to do it. Another such a brush, notwithstanding we lost the ground, would, by still reducing the enemy, put them in a condition to be afterwards totally defeated.

Could our whole army have come up to the attack at one time, the consequences had probably been otherwise; but our having different parts of the Brandywine-creek to guard, and the uncertainty which road to Philadelphia, the enemy would attempt to take, naturally afforded them an opportunity of passing with their main body at a place where only a part of ours could be posted; for it must strike every thinking man with conviction, that it requires a much greater force to oppose an enemy in several places, than is sufficient to defeat in any one place.

Men who are sincere in defending their freedom, will always feel concern at every circumstance which seems to make against them; it is the natural and honest consequence of all affectionate attachments, and the want of it is a vice. But the dejection lasts only for a moment; they soon rise out of it with additional vigor; the glow of hope, courage and fortitude, will, in a little time supply the place of every inferior passion and kindle the whole heart into heroism.

There is a mystery in the countenance of some causes, which we have not always present judgment enough to explain. It is distressing to see an enemy advancing into a country, but it is the only place in which we can beat them, and in which we have always beaten them, whenever they made the attempt. The nearer any disease approaches to a crisis, the nearer it is to a cure. Danger and deliverance make their advances together, and it is only the last push, that one or the other takes the lead.

There are many men who will do their duty when it is not wanted; but a genuine public spirit always appears most when there is most occasion for it. Thank God! our army though fatigued, is yet entire. The attack made by us yesterday, was under many disadvantages, naturally arising from the uncertainty of knowing which route the enemy would take; and from that circumstance, the whole of our force could not be brought up together time enough to engage all at once. Our strength is yet reserved; and it is evident that Howe does not think himself a gainer by the affair, otherwise he would this morning have moved down and attacked General Washington.

Gentlemen of the city and country, it is in your power, by a spirited improvement of the present circumstance, to turn it to a real advantage. Howe is now weaker than before, and every shot will contribute to reduce him. You are more immediately interested than any other part of the continent; your all is at stake; it is not so with the general cause; you are devoted by the enemy to plunder and destruction: It is the encouragement which Howe, the chief of plunderers, has promised his army. Thus circumstanced, you may save yourselves by a manly resistance, but you can have no hope in any other conduct. I never yet knew our brave general, or any part of the army, officers or men, out of heart, and I have seen them in circumstances a thousand times more trying than the present. It is only those that are not in action, that feel languor and heaviness, and the best way to rub it off is to turn out, and make sure work of it.

Our army must undoubtedly feel fatigue, and want a reinforcement of rest, though not of valor. Our own interest and happiness call upon us to give them every support in our power, and make the burden of the day, on which the safety of this city depends, light as possible. Remember, gentlemen, that we have forces both to the northward and southward of Philadelphia, and if the enemy be but stopt till those can arrive, this city will be saved, and the enemy finally routed. You have too much at stake to hesitate. You ought not to think an hour upon the matter, but to spring to action at once. Other states have been invaded, have likewise driven off the invaders. Now our time and turn is come, and perhaps the finishing stroke is reserved for us. When we look back on the dangers we have been saved from, and reflect on the success we have been blessed with, it would be sinful either to be idle or despair.

I close this paper with a short address to gen. Howe. You, sir, are only lingering out the period that shall bring with it your defeat, You have yet scarce began upon the war, and the farther you enter, the faster will your troubles thicken. What you now enjoy is only a respite from ruin; an invitation to destruction: something that will lead on to our deliverance at your expense. We know the cause we are engaged in, and though a passionate fondness for it may make us grieve at every injury that threatens it, yet, when the movement of concern is over, the determination to duty returns. We are not moved by the gloomy smile of a worthless king, but by the ardent glow of generous patriotism. We fight not to enslave, but to set a country free, and to make room upon the earth for honest men to live in. In such a cause we are sure we are right; and we leave to you the despairing reflection of being the tool of a miserable tyrant.

Number V

To General Sir William Howe

Lancaster, March 21, 1778

To argue with a man who has renounced the use and authority of reason, and whose philosophy consists in holding humanity in contempt, is like administering medicine to the dead, or endeavoring to convert an atheist by scripture. Enjoy, sir, your insensibility of feeling and reflecting. It is the prerogative of animals. And no man will envy you those honors, in which a savage only can be your rival and a bear your master.

As the generosity of this country rewarded your brother's services last war with an elegant monument in Westminster-Abbey, it is consistent that she should bestow some mark of distinction upon you. You certainly deserve her notice, and a conspicuous place in the catalogue of extraordinary persons. Yet it would be a pity to pass you from the world in state, and consign you to magnificent oblivion among the tombs, without telling the future beholder why. Judas is as much known as John, yet history ascribes their fame to very different actions.

Sir William hath undoubtedly merited a monument: But of what kind, or with what inscription, where placed or how embellished, is a question that would puzzle all the heralds of St. James' in the profoundest mood of historical deliberation. We are at no loss, sir, to ascertain your real character, but somewhat perplexed how to perpetuate its identity, and preserve it uninjured from the transformations of time or mistake. A statuary may give a false expression to your bust, or decorate it with some equivocal emblems, by which you may happen to steal into reputation and impose upon the hereafter traditionary world. Ill nature or ridicule may conspire, or a variety of accidents combine, to lessen, enlarge, or change Sir William's fame; and no doubt but he who has taken so much pains to be singular in his conduct, would choose to be just as singular in his exit, his monument and his epitaph.

The usual honors of the dead, to be sure, are not suf-

ficiently sublime to escort a character like you to the republic of dust and ashes; for however men may differ in
their ideas of grandeur or government here, the grave is
nevertheless a perfect republic. Death is not the monarch
of the dead, but of the dying. The moment he obtains a
conquest he loses a subject, and, like the foolish king you
serve, will, in the end, war himself out of all dominion.

As a proper preliminary towards the arrangement of
your funeral honors, we readily admit your new rank of
knighthood. The title is perfectly in character, and is your
own, more by merit than creation. There are knights of
various orders from the knight of the windmill to the
knight of the post. The former is your patron for exploits,
and the latter will assist you in settling your accounts. No
honorary title could be more happily applied! The inge-
nuity is sublime! And your royal master hath discovered
more genius in fitting you therewith, than in generating
the most finished figure for a button, or discanting on the
properties of a button-mould.

But how, sir, shall we dispose of you? The invention of
a statuary is exhausted, and Sir William is yet unprovided
with a monument. America is anxious to bestow her funeral favors upon you, and wishes to do it in a manner

that shall distinguish you from all the deceased heroes of the last war. The *Egyptian method of embalming* is not known to the present age, and hieroglyphical pageantry hath out-lived the science of decyphering it. Some other method, therefore, must be thought of to immortalize the new knight of the windmill and post. Sir William, thanks to his stars, is not oppressed with very delicate ideas. He has no ambition of being wrapt up and handed about in myrrh, aloes and cassia. Less chargeable odors will suffice; and it fortunately happens, that the simple genius of America hath discovered the art of preserving bodies and embellishing them too, with much greater frugality than the ancients. In a balmage, sir, of humble tar, you will be as secure as Pharoah, and in a hieroglyphic of feathers rival in finery all the mummies of Egypt.

As you have already made your exit from the moral world, and by numberless acts both of passionate and deliberate injustice engraved an "*Here Lyeth*" on your deceased honor, it must be more affectation in you to pretend concern at the humors or opinions of mankind respecting you. What remains of you may expire at any time. The sooner the better. For he who survives his reputation, lives out of spite to himself, like a man listening to his own reproach.

Thus entombed and ornamented I leave you to the inspection of the curious, and return to the history of your yet surviving actions.—The character of Sir William hath undergone some extraordinary revolutions since his arrival in America. It is now fixed and known; and we have nothing to hope from your candor or to fear from your capacity. Indolence and inability have too large a share in your composition ever to suffer you to be any thing more than the hero of little villanies and unfinished adventures. That, which to some persons appeared moderation in you at first, was not produced by any real virtue of your own, but by a contrast of passions dividing and holding you in perpetual irresolution. One vice will frequently expel another without the least merit in the man, as powers in contrary directions reduce each other to rest.

It became you to have supported a dignified solemnity of character; to have shewn a superior liberality of soul; to have won respect by an obstinate perseverance in maintaining order, and to have exhibited on all occasions, such an unchangeable graciousness of conduct, that while we beheld in you the resolution of an enemy, we might admire in you the sincerity of a man. You came to America under the high-sounding titles of commander and commissioner; not only to suppress what you called rebellion by arms, but to shame it out of countenance by the excellence of your example. Instead of which, you have been the patron of low and vulgar frauds, the encourager of Indian cruelties; and have imported a cargo of vices blacker than those you pretended to suppress.

Mankind are not universally agreed in their determination of right and wrong; but there are certain actions which the consent of all nations and individuals hath branded with the unchangeable name of MEANNESS. In the list of human vices we find some of such a refined constitution, that they cannot be carried into practice without seducing some virtue to their assistance; but *meanness* hath neither alliance nor apology. It is generated in the dust and sweepings of other vices, and is of such a hateful figure that all the rest conspire to disown it. Sir William, the commissioner of George the Third, hath at last vouchsafed to give it rank and pedigree. He has placed the fugitive at the council board, and dubbed it companion of the order of knighthood.

The particular act of meanness which I allude to in this

description, is forgery. You, sir, have abetted and patronized the forging and uttering counterfeit continental bills. In the same New-York newspapers in which your own proclamation under your master's authority was published, offering, or pretending to offer, pardon and protection to the inhabitants of these states, there were repeated advertisements of counterfeit money for sale, and persons who have come officially from you and under sanction of your flag, have been taken up in attempting to put them off.

A conduct so basely mean in a public character is without precedent or pretence, Every nation on earth, whether friends or enemies, will unite in despising you. 'Tis an incendiary war upon society which nothing can excuse or palliate—An improvement upon beggarly villany—and shews an inbred wretchedness of heart made up between the venomous malignity of a serpent and the spiteful imbecility of an inferior reptile.

The laws of any civilized country would condemn you to the gibbet without regard to your rank or titles, because it is an action foreign to the usage and custom of war; and should you fall into our hands, which pray God you may, it will be a doubtful matter whether we are to consider you as a military prisoner or a prisoner for felony.

Besides, it is exceedingly unwise and impolitic in you, or any persons in the English service, to promote, or even encourage, or wink, at the crime of forgery in any case whatever. Because, as the riches of England, as a nation, are chiefly in paper, and the far greater part of trade among individuals is carried on by the same medium, that is, by notes and drafts on one another, they, therefore, of all people in the world ought to endeavor to keep forgery out of sight, and, if possible, not to revive the idea of it. It is dangerous to make men familiar with a crime which they may afterwards practise to much greater advantage against those who first taught them. Several officers in the English army have made their exit at the gallows for forgery on their agents; for we all know, who know any thing of England, that there is not a more necessitous body of men, taking them generally, than what the English officers are. They contrive to make a shew at the expence of the taylor, and appear clean at the charge of the washer-woman.

England hath at this time nearly two hundred million pounds sterling of public money in paper, for which she

34

hath no real property, besides a large circulation of bank notes, bank post bills, and promissory notes and drafts of private bankers, merchants and tradesmen. She hath the greatest quantity of paper currency and the least quantity of gold and silver of any nation in Europe; the real specie, which is about sixteen millions sterling, serve only as change in large sums, which are always made in paper, or for payment in small ones. Thus circumstanced, the nation is put to its wit's end, and obliged to be severe almost to criminality, to prevent the practice and growth of forgery. Scarcely a session passes at the Old Bailey, or an execution at Tyburn, but witnesseth this truth. Yet you, sir, regardless of the policy which her necessity obliges her to adopt, have made your whole army intimate with the crime. And as all armies, at the conclusion of a war, are too apt to carry into practice the vices of the campaign, it will probably happen, that England will hereafter abound in forgeries, to which art, the practitioners were first initiated under your authority in America. You, sir, have the honor of adding a new vice to the military catalogue; and the reason, perhaps, why the invention was reserved for you is, because no General before that was mean enough even to think of it.

That a man whose soul is absorbed in the low traffic of vulgar vice, is incapable of moving in any superior region, is clearly shewn in you by the event of every campaign. Your military exploits have been without plan, object or decision. Can it be possible that you or your employers can suppose the possession of Philadelphia to be any ways equal to the expence or expectation of the nation which supports you? What advantages does England derive from any achievements of yours? To *her* it is perfectly indifferent what place you are in, so long as the business of conquest is unperformed and the charge of maintaining you remains the same.

If the principal events of the three campaigns be attended to, the balance will appear strongly against you at the close of each; but the last, in point of importance to us, hath exceeded the former two. It is pleasant to look back on dangers past, and equally as pleasant to meditate on present ones when the way out begins to appear. *That* period is now arrived, and the long doubtful winter of war is changing to the sweeter prospects of victory and joy. At the close of the campaign in seventy-five, you were obliged to retreat from Boston. In the summer of seventy-six, you appeared with a numerous fleet and army in the harbor of New-York. By what miracle the Continent was preserved in that season of danger is a subject of admiration! If instead of wasting your time against Long-Island, you had run up the North-River and landed any where above New-York, the consequence must have been, that either you would have compelled General Washington to fight you with very unequal numbers, or he must have suddenly evacuated the city with the loss of nearly all the stores of the army, or have surrendered for want of provisions, the situation of the place naturally producing one or other of these events.

The preparations made to defend New-York were, nevertheless, wise and military; because your forces were then at sea, their numbers uncertain; storms, sickness, or a variety of accidents must have disabled their coming, or so diminished them on their passage, that those which survived would have been incapable of opening the campaign with any prospect of success; in which case, the defence would have been sufficient and the place preserved; for cities that have been raised from nothing with an infinitude of labor and expence, are not to be thrown away on the bare probability of their being taken. On these grounds, the preparations made to maintain New-

York were as judicious as the retreat afterwards. While you, in the interim, let slip the *very* opportunity which seemed to put conquest in your power.

Through the whole of that campaign you had nearly double the forces which General Washington immediately commanded. The principal plan, at that time, on our part, was to wear away the season with as little loss as possible, and to raise the army for the next year. Long-Island, New-York, Forts Washington and Lee were not defended, after your superior force was known, under any expectation of their being finally maintained, but as a range of out works, in the attacking of which, your time might be wasted, your numbers reduced, and your vanity amused by possessing them on our retreat. It was intended to have withdrawn the garrison from Fort Washington after it had answered the former of those purposes, but the fate of that day put a prize into your hands without much honor to yourselves.

Your progress through the Jerseys was accidental; you had it not even in contemplation, or you would not have sent so principal a part of your force to Rhode-Island before-hand. The utmost hope of America in the year seventy-six reached no higher than that she might not *then* be conquered. She had no expectation of defeating you in that campaign. Even the most cowardly tory allowed, that, could she withstand the shock of *that* summer her independence would be past a doubt. You had *then* greatly the advantage of her. You were formidable. Your military knowledge was supposed to be complete. Your fleets and forces arrived without an accident. You had neither experience nor reinforcements to wait for. You had nothing to do but to begin, and your chance lay in the first vigorous onset.

America was young and unskilled. She was obliged to trust her defence to time and practice; and hath, by mere dint of perseverance, maintained her cause, and brought her enemy to a condition, in which, she is now capable of meeting him on any grounds.

It is remarkable that in the campaign of seventy-six, you gained no more, notwithstanding your great force than what was given you by consent of evacuation, except Fort Washington: While every advantage obtained by us was by fair and hard fighting. The defeat of Sir Peter Parker was complete. The conquest of the Hessions at Trenton by the remains of a retreating army, which but a few days before, you affected to despise, is an instance of heroic perseverance very seldom to be met with. And the victory over the British troops at Princeton, by a harassed and wearied party, who had been engaged the day before and marched all night without refreshment, is attended with such a scene of circumstances and superiority of generalship, as will ever give it a place on the first line in the history of great actions.

When I look back on the gloomy days of last winter and see America suspended by a thread, I feel a triumph of joy at the recollection of her delivery, and a reverence for the characters which snatched her from destruction. To doubt *now* would be a species of infidelity, and to forget the instruments which saved us *then* would be ingratitude.

The close of that campaign left us with the spirits of conquerors. The northern districts were relieved by the retreat of General Carleton over the lakes. The army under your command were hunted back and had their bounds prescribed. The Continent began to feel its military importance, and the winter passed pleasantly away in preparations for the next campaign.

However confident you might be on your first arrival, the course of the year seventy-six gave you some idea of the difficulty, if not impossibility, of conquest. To this reason I ascribe your delay in opening the campaign in seventy-seven. The face of matters, on the close of the former year, gave you no encouragement to pursue a discretionary war as soon as the spring admitted the taking the field: for though conquest, in that case, would have given you a double portion of fame, yet the experiment was too hazardous. The ministry, had you failed, would have shifted the whole blame upon you, charged you with having acted without orders, and condemned at once both your plan and your execution.

To avoid those misfortunes, which might have involved you and your money accounts in perplexity and suspicion, you prudently waited the arrival of a plan of operations from England, which was, that you should proceed for Philadelphia by way of Chesapeake, and that Burgoyne, after reducing Ticonderoga, should take his route by Albany, and, if necessary, join you.

The splendid laurels of the last campaign have flourished in the north. In that quarter America hath surprized the world, and laid the foundation of her this year's glory. The conquest of Ticonderoga (if it may be called a conquest) has, like all your other victories, led on to ruin. Even the provisions taken in that fortress, (which by General Burgoyne's return was sufficient in bread and flour for nearly 5000 men for ten weeks, and in beef and pork for the same number of men for one month) served only to hasten his overthrow, by enabling him to proceed for Saratoga the place of his destruction. A short review of the operations of the last campaign will shew the condition of affairs on both sides.

You have taken Ticonderoga and marched into Philadelphia. These are all the events which the year hath produced on your part. A trifling campaign indeed, compared with the expences of England and the conquest of the continent. On the other side, a considerable part of your northern force has been routed by the New-York militia under General Herkemer. Fort Stanwix hath bravely survived a compounded attack of soldiers and savages, and the besiegers have fled. The battle of Bennington has put a thousand prisoners into our hands, with all their arms, stores, artillery and baggage. General Burgoyne in two engagements has been defeated; himself, his army, and all that were his and theirs are now ours. Ticonderoga and Independence are retaken, and not the shadow of an enemy remains in all the northern districts. At this instant we have upwards of eleven thousand prisoners, between sixty and seventy pieces of brass ordnance, besides small arms, tents, stores, &c. &c.

In order to know the real value of those advantages we must reverse the scene, and suppose General Gates and the force he commanded, to be at your mercy as prisoners, and General Burgoyne with his army of soldiers and savages to be already joined to you in Pennsylvania. So dismal a picture can scarcely be looked at. It hath all the traces and colourings of horror and despair; and excites the most swelling emotions of gratitude by exhibiting the miseries we are so graciously preserved from.

I admire this distribution of laurels around the continent. It is the earnest of future union. South-Carolina has had her day of suffering and of fame; and the other southern states have exerted themselves in proportion to the force that invaded or insulted them. Towards the close of the campaign in seventy-six, these middle states were called upon and did their duty nobly. They were witnesses to the almost expiring flame of human freedom. It was the close struggle of life and death. The line of invisible division; and on which, the unabated fortitude of a

Washington prevailed, and saved the spark, that has since blazed in the north with unrivalled lustre.

Let me ask, sir, what great exploits have you performed? Through all the variety of changes and opportunities which this war hath produced, I know no one action of yours that can be stiled masterly. You have moved in and out, backward and forward, round and round, as if valor consisted in a military jig. The history and figure of your movements would be truly ridiculous could they be justly delineated. They resemble the labors of a puppy pursuing his tail; the end is still at the same distance, and all the turnings round must be done over again.

The first appearance of affairs at Ticonderoga wore such an unpromising aspect, that it was necessary, in July, to detach a part of the forces to the support of that quarter, which were otherwise destined or intended to act against you, and this, perhaps, has been the means of postponing your downfal to another campaign. The destruction of one army at a time is work enough. We know, sir, what we are about, what we have to do, and how to do it.

Your progress from Chesapeake was marked by no

capital stroke of policy or heroism. Your principal aim was to get General Washington between the Delaware and Schuylkill and between Philadelphia and your army. In that situation, with a river on each of his flanks, which united about five miles below the city, and your army above him, you could have intercepted his reinforcements and supplies, cut off all his communication with the country, and, if necessary, have dispatched assistance to open a passage for General Burgoyne. This scheme was too visible to succeed, for had General Washington suffered you to command the open country above him, I think it a very reasonable conjecture that the conquest of Burgoyne would not have taken place, because you could, in that case, have relieved him. It was therefore necessary, while that important victory was in suspence, to trepan *you* into a situation, in which you could only be on the defensive without the power of affording him assistance. The manoeuvre had its effect and Burgoyne was conquered.

There has been something unmilitarily passive in you from the time of your passing the Schuylkill and getting possession of Philadelphia to the close of the campaign. You mistook a trap for a conquest, the probability of which had been made known to Europe, and the edge of your triumph taken off by our own information long before.

Having got you into this situation, a scheme for a general attack upon you at Germantown was carried into execution on the fourth of October, and though the success was not equal to the excellence of the plan, yet the attempting it proved the genius of America to be on the rise and her power approaching to superiority. The obscurity of the morning was your best friend, for a fog is always favorable to a hunted enemy. Some weeks after this, you, likewise, planned an attack on General Washington while at Whitemarsh. Marched out with infinite parade, but on finding him preparing to attack you the next morning, you prudently cut about and retreated to Philadelphia with all the precipitation of a man conquered in imagination.

Immediately after the battle of Germantown, the probability of Burgoyne's defeat gave a new policy to affairs in Pennsylvania, and it was judged most consistent with the general safety of America to wait the issue of the Northern campaign. Slow and sure is sound work. The news of that victory arrived in our camp on the 18th of October, and no sooner did the shout of joy and the report of the thirteen cannon reach your ears, than you resolved upon a retreat, and the next day, that is, on the 19th, withdrew your drooping army into Philadelphia. This movement was evidently dictated by fear; and carried with it a positive confession that you dreaded a second attack. It was hiding yourself among women and children, and sleeping away the choicest part of a campaign in expensive inactivity. An army in a city can never be a conquering army. The situation admits only of defence. It is mere shelter; and every military power in Europe will conclude you to be eventually defeated.

The time when you made this retreat was the very time you ought to have fought a battle, in order to put yourself in a condition of recovering in Pennsylvania what you had lost at Saratoga. And the reason why you did not, must be either prudence or cowardice; the former supposes your inability, and the latter needs no explanation. I draw no conclusions, sir, but such as are naturally deduced from known and visible facts, and such as will always have a being while the facts which produced them remain unaltered.

After this retreat a new difficulty arose which exhibited

the power of Britain in a very contemptible light, which was the attack and defence of Mud-Island. For several weeks did that little unfinished fortress stand out against all the attempts of Admiral and General Howe. It was the fable of Bendar realized on the Delaware. Scheme after scheme, and force upon force were tried and defeated. The garrison, with scarce any thing to cover them but their bravery, survived in the midst of mud, shot and shells, and were at last obliged to give it up more to the powers of time and gun-powder than to the military superiority of the besiegers.

It is my sincere opinion that matters are in a much worse condition with you than what is generally known. Your master's speech at the opening of parliament is like a soliloquy on ill luck. It shews him to be coming a little to his reason, for sense of pain is the first symptom of recovery in profound stupefactions. His condition is deplorable. He is obliged to submit to all the insults of France and Spain without daring to know or resent them, and thankful for the most trivial evasions to the most humble remonstrances. The time *was* when he could not *deign* an answer to a petition from America, and the time now *is* when he dare not *give* an answer to an affront from

France. The capture of Burgoyne's army will sink his consequence as much in Europe as in America. In his speech he expresses his suspicions at the warlike preparations of France and Spain, and as he has only the one army which you command to support his character in the world with, it remains very uncertain when, or in what quarter, it will be most wanted or can be best employed; and this will partly account for the great care you take to keep it from action and attacks, for should Burgoyne's fate be yours, which it probably will, England may take her endless farewel not only of all America but of all the West-Indies.

Never did a nation invite destruction upon itself with the eagerness and ignorance with which Britain has done. Bent upon the ruin of a young and unoffending country, she hath drawn the sword that hath wounded herself to the heart, and in the agony of her resentment hath applied a poison for a cure. Her conduct towards America is a compound of rage and lunacy; she aims at her government of it, yet preserves neither dignity nor character in her methods to obtain it. Were government a mere manufacture or article of commerce immaterial by whom it should be made or sold, we might as well employ her as another, but when we consider it as the fountain from whence the general manners and morality of a country take their rise, that the persons entrusted with the execution thereof are by their serious example and authority to support these principles, how abominably absurd is the idea of being hereafter governed by a set of men who have been guilty of forgery, perjury, treachery, theft, and every species of villany which the lowest wretches on earth could practise or invent. What greater public curse can befal any country than to be delivered therefrom. The soul of any man of sentiment would rise in brave rebellion against them and spurn them from the earth.

The malignant and venomous tempered General Vaughan has amused his savage fancy in burning the whole town of Kingston, in York government, and the late Governor of that State, Mr. Tryon, in his letter to General Parsons, has endeavored to justify it, and declared his wish to burn the houses of every committee-man in the country. Such a confession from one who was once entrusted with the powers of civil government, is a reproach to the character. But it is the wish and the declaration of a man whom anguish and disappointment have driven to despair, and who is daily decaying into the grave with constitutional rottenness.

There is not in the compass of language a sufficiency of words to express the baseness of your king, his ministry and his army. They have refined upon villany till it wants a name. To the fiercer vices of former ages they have added the dregs and scummings of the most finished rascality, and are so completely sunk in serpentine deceit, that there is not left among them *one* generous enemy.

From such men and such masters may the gracious hand of Heaven preserve America! And though the sufferings she now endures are heavy and severe, they are like straws in the wind compared to the weight of evils she would feel under the government of your king, and his pensioned parliament.

There is something in meanness which excites a species of resentment that never subsides, and something in cruelty which stirs up the heart to the highest agony of human hatred; Britain hath filled up both these characters till no addition can be made, and hath not reputation left with us to obtain credit for the slightest promise. The will of God hath parted us, and the deed is registered for eternity. When she shall be a spot scarcely visible among the nations, America shall flourish the favorite of Heaven and the friend of mankind.

For the domestic happiness of Britain and the peace of the world I wish she had not a foot of land but what is circumscribed within her own island. Extent of dominion hath been her ruin, and instead of civilizing others hath brutalized herself. Her late reduction of India, under Clive and his successors, was not so properly a conquest as an extermination of mankind. She is the only power who could practise the prodigal barbarity of tying men to the mouths of loaded cannon and blowing them away. It happens that General Burgoyne, who made the report of that horrid transaction in the house of commons, is now a prisoner with us, and though an enemy, I can appeal to him for the truth of it, being confident that he neither can nor will deny it. Yet Clive received the approbation of the last parliament.

When we take a survey of mankind we cannot help cursing the wretch, who, to the unavoidable misfortunes of nature shall wilfully add the calamities of war. One would think there were evils enough in the world without studying to increase them, and that life is sufficiently short without shaking the sand that measure it. The histories of Alexander, and Charles of Sweden, are the histories of human devils; a good man cannot think of their actions without abhorrence nor of their deaths without rejoicings. To see the bounties of Heaven destroyed, the beautiful face of nature laid waste, and the choicest works of creation and art tumbled into ruin, would fetch a curse from the soul of piety itself. But in this country the aggravation is heightened by a new combination of affecting circumstances. America was young, and, compared with other countries, was virtuous. None but a Herod of uncommon malice would have made war upon infancy and innocence, and none but a people of the most finished fortitude dared, under those circumstances, have resisted the tyranny. The natives, or their ancestors, had fled from the former oppressions of England, and with the industry of bees had changed a wilderness into a habitable world. To Britain they were indebted for nothing. The country was the gift of Heaven, and God alone is their Lord and Sovereign.

The time, sir, will come when you, in a melancholy hour, shall reckon up your miseries by your murders in America. Life, with you, begins to wear a clouded aspect. The vision of pleasurable delusion is wearing away, and changing to the barren wild of age and sorrow. The poor reflection of having served your king will yield you no consolation in your parting moments. He will crumble to the same undistinguished ashes with yourself, and have sins enough of his own to answer for. It is not the farcical benedictions of a bishop, nor the cringing hypocrisy of a court of chaplains, nor the formality of an act of parliament, that can change guilt into innocence, or make the punishment *one* pang the less. You may, perhaps, be unwilling to be serious, but this destruction of the goods of Providence, this havoc of the human race, and this sowing the world with mischief, must be accounted for to him who made and governs it. To us they are only present sufferings, but to him they are deep rebellions.

If there is a sin superior to every other it is that of wilful and offensive war. Most other sins are circumscribed within narrow limits, that is, the power of *one* man cannot give them a very general extension, and many kind of sins have only a mental existence from which no infection arises; but he who is the author of a war, lets loose the whole contagion of hell, and opens a vein that bleeds a nation to death. We leave it to England and Indians to boast of these honors; we feel no thirst for such savage glory; a nobler flame, a purer spirit animates America. She hath taken up the sword of virtuous defence; she hath bravely put herself between Tyranny and Freedom, between a curse and a blessing, determined to expel the one, and protect the other.

It is the object only of war that makes it honorable. And if there were ever a *just* war since the world began, it is this which America is now engaged in. She invaded no land of yours. She hired no mercenaries to burn your towns, nor Indians to massacre their inhabitants. She wanted nothing from you and was indebted for nothing to you; and thus circumstanced, her defence is honorable and her prosperity certain.

Yet it is not on the *justice* only, but likewise on the *importance* of this cause that I ground my seeming enthusiastical confidence of our success. The vast extension of America makes her of too much value in the scale of Providence, to be cast, like a pearl before swine, at the feet of an European island; and of much less consequence would it be that Britain were sunk in the sea than that America should miscarry. There has been such a chain of extraordinary events in the discovery of this country at first, in the peopling and planting it afterwards, in the rearing and nursing it to its present state, and in the protection of it through the present war, that no man can doubt, but Providence hath some nobler end to accomplish than the gratification of the petty elector of Hanover or the ignorant and insignificant king of Britain.

As the blood of the martyrs hath been the seed of the Christian church, so the political persecutions of England will and hath already enriched America with industry, experience, union and importance. Before the present æra she was a mere chaos of uncemented Colonies, individually exposed to the ravages of the Indians and the invasion of any power that Britain should be at war with. She had nothing she could call her own. Her felicity depended upon accident. The convulsions of Europe might have thrown her from one conqueror to another, till she had been the slave of all and ruined by every one; for until she had spirit enough to become her own master, there was no knowing to which master she should belong. *That* period, thank God, is past, and she is no longer the dependant, disunited Colonies of Britain, but the independent and United States of America, knowing no master but Heaven and herself. You or your king may call this "Delusion," "Rebellion," or what name you please. To us it is perfectly indifferent. The issue will determine the character and time will give it a name as lasting as his own.

You have now, sir, tried the fate of three campaigns, and can fully declare to England, that nothing is to be got on your part but blows and broken bones, and nothing on hers but waste of trade and credit and an encrease of poverty and taxes. You are now only where you might have been two years ago without the loss of a single ship, and yet not a step the forwarder towards the conquest of the Continent; because, as I have already hinted, "An army in a city can never be a conquering army." The full amount of your losses since the beginning of the war exceeds twenty thousand men, besides millions of treasure for which you have nothing in exchange. Our expences, though great, are circulated within ourselves. Yours is a direct sinking of money, and that from both ends at once, first in hiring troops out of the nation, and in paying them afterwards, because the money in neither case can return again to Britain. We are already in possession of the prize, you only in suit for it. To us it is a real treasure, to you it would be only an empty triumph. Our expences will repay themselves with ten fold interest, while yours entail upon you everlasting property.

Take a review, sir, of the ground you have gone over,

and let it teach you policy, if it cannot honesty. You stand but on a very tottering foundation. A change of the ministry in England may probably bring your measures into question and your head to the block. Clive, with all his successes, had some difficulty in escaping, and yours being all a war of losses, will afford you less pretensions and your enemies more grounds for impeachment.

Go home, sir, and endeavor to save the remains of your ruined country by a just representation of the madness of her measures. A few moments well applied may yet preserve her from political destruction. I am not one of those who wish to see Europe in a flame, because I am persuaded such an event will not shorten the war. The rupture, at present, is confined between the two powers of America and England. England finds she cannot conquer America, and America has no wish to conquer England. You are fighting for what you can never obtain, and we defending what we mean never to part with. A few words, therefore, settle the bargain. Let England mind her own business and we will mind ours. Govern yourselves and we will govern ourselves. You may then trade where you please unmolested by us, and we will trade where we please unmolested by you; and such articles as we can purchase of each other better than elsewhere may be mutually done. If it were possible that you could carry on the war for twenty years you must still come to this point at last, or worse, and the sooner you think of it the better it will be for you.

My official situation enables me to know the repeated insults which Britain is obliged to put up with from foreign powers, and the wretched shifts she is driven to, to gloss them over. Her reduced strength and exhausted coffers in a three years' war with America had given a powerful superiority to France and Spain. She is not now a match for them—But if neither counsels can prevail on her to think, nor sufferings awaken her to reason, she must e'en go on, till the honor of England becomes a proverb of contempt, and Europe dub her the Land of Fools.

    I am, Sir,

        With every wish for an honorable peace,

            Your friend, enemy, and countryman,

                COMMON SENSE

To the Inhabitants of America

With all the pleasure with which a man exchanges bad company for good, I take my leave of Sir William and return to you. It is now nearly three years since the tyranny of Britain received its first repulse by the arms of America. A period, which has given birth to a new world and erected a monument to the folly of the old.

I cannot help being sometimes surprised at the complimentary references which I have seen and heard made to ancient histories and transactions. The wisdom, civil governments, and sense of honor of the States of Greece and Rome, are frequently held up as objects of excellence and imitation. Mankind have lived for very little purpose, if, at this period of the world, they must go two or three thousand years back for lessons and examples. We do dishonorary injustice to ourselves by placing them in such a superior line. We have no just authority for it, neither can we tell why it is that we should suppose ourselves inferior.

Could the mist of antiquity be taken away, and men and

things viewed as they then really were, it is more than probable that they would admire us, rather than we them. America has surmounted a greater variety and combination of difficulties than, I believe, ever fell to the share of any one people in the same space of time, and has replenished the world with more useful knowledge and sounder maxims of civil government than were ever produced in any age before. Had it not been for America there had been no such thing as freedom left throughout the whole universe. England hath lost hers in a long chain of right reasoning from wrong principles, and it is from this country now she must learn the resolution to redress herself, and the wisdom how.

The Grecians and Romans were strongly possessed of the *Spirit* of liberty but *not* the *principle*, for at the time they were determined not to be slaves themselves, they employed their power to enslave the rest of mankind. But this distinguished area is blotted by no one misanthropical vice. In short, if the principle on which the cause is founded, the universal blessings that are to arise from it, the difficulties that accompanied it, the wisdom with which it has been debated, the fortitude by which it has been supported, the strength of the power we had to oppose, and the condition in which we undertook it, be all taken in one view, we may justly stile it the most virtuous and illustrious revolution that ever graced the history of mankind.

A good opinion of ourselves is exceedingly necessary in private life, but absolutely necessary in public life, and of the utmost importance in supporting national character. I have no notion of yielding the palm of the United States to any Grecians or Romans that were ever born. We have equalled the bravest in times of danger, and excelled the wisest in the construction of civil governments, *no one in America excepted.*

From this agreeable eminence let us take a review of present affairs. The spirit of corruption is so inseparably interwoven with British politics, that their ministry suppose all mankind are governed by the same motive. They have no idea of a people submitting even to temporary inconvenience from an attachment to rights and privileges. Their plans of business are calculated *by* the hour and *for* the hour, and are uniform in nothing but the corruption which gives them birth. They never had, neither have they at this time, any regular plan for the conquest of America by arms. They know not how to go about it, neither have they power to effect it if they could know. The thing is not within the compass of human practicability, for America is too extensive either to be fully conquered or *passively* defended. But she may be *actively* defended by defeating or making prisoners of the army that invades her. And this is the only system of defence that can be effectual in a large country.

There is something in a war carried on by invasion which makes it differ in circumstances from any other mode of war, because he who conducts it cannot tell whether the ground he gains, be for him, or against him, when he first makes it. In the winter of seventy-six General Howe marched with an air of victory through the Jerseys, the consequence of which was his defeat, and General Burgoyne at Saratoga experienced the same fate from the same cause. The Spaniards about two years ago were defeated by the Algerines in the same manner, that is, their first triumphs became a trap in which they were totally routed. And whoever will attend to the circumstances and events of a war carried on by invasion, will find, that any invader, in order to be finally conquered must first begin to conquer.

I confess myself one of those who believe the loss of

Philadelphia to be attended with more advantages than injuries. The case stood thus. The enemy imagined Philadelphia to be of more importance to us than it really was; for we all know that it had long ceased to be a port, not a cargo of goods had been brought into it for near a twelve-month, nor any fixed manufactories, not even ship-building carried on in it; yet as the enemy believed the conquest of it to be practicable, and to that belief added the absurd idea that the soul of all America was centered there, and would be conquered there, it naturally follows, that their possession of it, by not answering the end proposed, must break up the plans they had so foolishly gone upon, and either oblige them to form a new one, for which their present strength is not sufficient, or to give over the attempt.

We never had so small an army to fight against, nor so fair an opportunity of final success as *now*. The death wound is already given. The day is our own if we follow it up. The enemy by his situation is within our reach, and by his reduced strength is within our power. The ministers of Britain may rage as they please, but our part is to conquer their armies. Let them wrangle and welcome, but let it not draw our attention from the *one* thing needful.

Here, in this spot is our business to be accomplished, our felicity secured. What we have now to do is as clear as light, and the way to do it is as strait as a line. It needs not to be commented upon, yet, in order to be perfectly understood I will put a case that cannot admit of a mistake.

Had the armies under the Generals Howe and Burgoyne been united and taken post at Germantown, and had the Northern army, under General Gates been joined to that under General Washington at Whitemarsh, the consequence would have been a general action; and if in the action we had killed and taken the same number of officers and men, that is, between nine and ten thousand, with the same quantity of artillery, arms, stores, &c. as have been taken at the Northward, and obliged General Howe with the remains of his army, that is, with the same number he now commands, to take shelter in Philadelphia, we should certainly have thought ourselves the greatest heroes in the world; and should, as soon as the season permitted, have collected together all the force of the Continent and laid siege to the city, for it requires a much greater force to besiege an enemy in a town than to defeat them in the field. The case *now* is just the same as if it had been produced by the means I have here supposed. Between nine and ten thousand have been killed and taken, all their stores are in our possession, and General Howe, in consequence of that victory, has thrown himself for shelter into Philadelphia. He, or his trifling friend Galloway, may form what pretences they please, yet no just reason can be given for their going into winter quarters so early as the 19th of October, but their apprehension of a defeat if they continued out, or their conscious inability of keeping the field with safety. I see no advantage which can arise to America by hunting the enemy from state to state. It is a triumph without a prize, and wholly unworthy the attention of a people determined to conquer. Neither can any state promise itself security while the enemy remains in a condition to transport themselves from one part of the Continent to another. Howe, likewise, cannot conquer where we have no army to oppose, therefore any such removals in him are mean and cowardly, and reduces Britain to a common pilferer. If he retreats from Philadelphia, he will be despised; if he stays, he may be shut up and starved out, and the country, if he advances into it, may become his Saratoga. He has his choice of evils and we of opportunities. If he moves early, it is not only a sign but a proof that he expects no reinforcement, and his delays will prove that he either waits for the arrival of a plan to go upon, or force to execute it, or both; in *which* case, our strength will increase more than his, therefore in *any* case we cannot be wrong if we do but proceed.

The particular condition of Pennsylvania deserves the attention of all the other states. Her military strength must not be estimated by the number of inhabitants. Here are men of all nations, characters, professions and interests. Here are the firmest whigs, surviving, like sparks in the ocean, unquenched and uncooled in the midst of discouragement and disaffection. Here are men losing their all with cheerfulness, and collecting fire and fortitude from the flames of their own estates. Here are others skulking in secret, many making a market of the times, and numbers who are changing whig and tory with the circumstances of every day.

It is by mere dint of fortitude and perseverance that the whigs of this state have been able to maintain so good a countenance, and do even what they have done. We want help, and the sooner it can arrive the more effectual it will be. The invaded state, be it which it may, will always feel an additional burthen upon its back, and be hard set to support its civil power with sufficient authority: and this difficulty will always rise or fall, in proportion as the other states throw in their assistance to the common cause.

The enemy will most probably make many manoeuvres at the opening of this campaign, to amuse and draw off the attention of the several states from the *one thing needful*. We may expect to hear of alarms and pretended expeditions to *this* place and *that* place, to the Southward, the Eastward and the Northward, all intended to prevent our forming into one formidable body. The less the enemy's strength is, the more subtleties of this kind will they make use of. Their existence depends upon it, because the force of America, when collected, is sufficient to swallow their present army up. It is therefore our business to make short work of it, by bending our whole attention to *this one principal point*, for the instant that the main body under General Howe is defeated, all the inferior alarms thro'out the Continent, like so many shadows, will follow his downfal.

The only way to finish a war with the least possible bloodshed, or perhaps without any, is to collect an army, against the power of which, the enemy shall have no chance. By not doing this, we prolong the war, and double both the calamities and the expences of it. What a rich and happy country would America be, were she, by a vigorous exertion, to reduce Howe as she has reduced Burgoyne. Her currency would rise to millions beyond its present value. Every man would be rich, and every man would have it in his power to be happy. And why not do these things? What is there to hinder? America is her own mistress and can do what she pleases.

If we had not at this time a man in the field, we could, nevertheless, raise an army in a few weeks sufficient to overwhelm all the force which General Howe at present commands. Vigor and determination will do any thing and every thing. We began the war with this kind of spirit, why not end it with the same? Here, gentlemen, is the enemy. Here is the army. The interest, the happiness, of all America is centered in this half ruined spot. Come on and help us. Here are laurels, come and share them. Here are tories, come and help us to expel them. Here are whigs that will make you welcome, and enemies that dread your coming.

The worst of all policy is that of doing things by

halves. Penny wise and pound foolish, has been the ruin of thousands. The present spring, if rightly improved, will free us from all our troubles, and save us the expence of millions. We have now only one army to cope with. No opportunity can be fairer; no prospect more promising. I shall conclude this paper with a few outlines of a plan, either for filling up the battalions with expedition, or for raising an additional force, for any limited time, on any sudden emergency.

That in which every man is interested, is every man's duty to support. And any burthen which falls equally on all men, and, from which every man is to receive an equal benefit, is consistent with the most perfect ideas of liberty. I would wish to revive something of that virtuous ambition which first called America into the field. Then every man was eager to do his part, and perhaps the principal reason why we have in any degree fallen therefrom, is, because we did not set a sufficient value by it at first, but left it to blaze out of itself, instead of regulating and preserving it by just proportions of rest and service.

Suppose any state whose number of effective inhabitants was 80,000 should be required to furnish 3,200 men towards the defence of the Continent, on any sudden emergency.

First, Let the whole number of effective inhabitants be divided into hundreds; then if each of those hundreds turn out four men, the whole number of 3,200 will be had.

Secondly, Let the names of each hundred men be entered in a book, and let four dollars be collected from each man, with as much more as any of the gentlemen, whose abilities can afford it, shall please to throw in, which gifts shall likewise be entered against the donors names.

Thirdly, Let the sums so collected be offered as a present, over and above the bounty of twenty dollars, to any four who may be enclined to propose themselves as volunteers; if more than four offer, the majority of the subscribers present shall determine which; if none offer, then four out of the hundred shall be taken by lot, who shall be entitled to the said sums, and shall either go, or provide others that will, in the space of six days.

Fourthly, As it will always happen, that in the space of ground on which an hundred men shall live, there will be always a number of persons who, by age and infirmity, are incapable of doing personal service, and as such persons are generally possessed of the greatest part of the property in any county, their portion of service, therefore, will be to furnish each man with a blanket, which will make a regimental coat, jacket and breeches, or cloaths in lieu thereof, and another for a watch cloak, and two pair of shoes—for however choice people may be of these things matters not in cases of this kind—Those who live always in houses can find many ways to keep themselves warm, but it is a shame and a sin to suffer a soldier in the field to want a blanket while there is one in the country.

Should the cloathing not be wanted, the superannuated or infirm persons possessing property, may, in lieu thereof, throw in their money subscriptions towards increasing the bounty, for though age will naturally exempt a person from personal service, it cannot exempt him from his share of the charge, because the men are raised for the defence of property and liberty, jointly.

There never was a scheme against which objections might not be raised. But this alone is not a sufficient reason for rejection. The only line to judge truly upon, is, to draw out and admit all the objections which can fairly be made, and place against them all the contrary qualities, conveniences and advantages, then by striking a balance you come at the true character of any scheme, principle or position.

The most material advantages of the plan here proposed are ease, expedition, and cheapness; yet the men so raised get a much larger bounty than is any where at present given; because all the expences, extravagance, and consequent idleness of recruiting are saved or prevented. The country incurs no new debt, nor interest thereon; the whole matter being all settled at once and entirely done with. It is a subscription answering all the purposes of a tax, without either the charge or trouble of collecting. The men are ready for the field with the greatest possible expedition, because it becomes the duty of the inhabitants themselves, in every part of the country, to find up their proportion of men, instead of leaving it to a recruiting sergeant, who, be he ever so industrious, cannot know always where to apply.

I do not propose this as a regular digested plan, neither will the limits of this paper admit of any further remarks upon it. I believe it to be a hint capable of much improvement, and as such submit it to the public.

Number VII (Selections)

To the People of England

Philadelphia, Nov. 21, 1778

. . . a set of very interesting and rational questions.

First, What is the original fountain of power and honor in any country?

Secondly, Whether the prerogative does not belong to the people?

Thirdly, Whether there is any such thing as the English constitution?

Fourthly, Of what use is the crown to the people?

Fifthly, Whether he who invented a crown was not an enemy to mankind?

Sixthly, Whether it is not a shame for a man to spend a million a year and do no good for it, and whether the money might not be better applied?

Seventhly, Whether such a man is not better dead than alive?

Eighthly, Whether a congress constituted like that of America, is not the most happy and consistent form of government in the world? . . .

Number VIII (Selections)

Addressed to the People of England

. . . Make but the case of others your own, and your own theirs, and you will then have a clear idea of the whole. Had France acted towards her colonies as you have done, you would have branded her with every epithet of abhorrence; and had you like her, stept in to succour a struggling people, all Europe must have echoed with your own applauses. But entangled in the passion of dispute, you see it not as you ought, and form opinions thereon which suit with no interest but your own. You wonder America does not rise in union with you to impose on herself a portion of your taxes and reduce herself to unconditional submission. You are amazed that the southern powers of Europe do not assist you in conquering a country which is afterwards to be turned against themselves; and that the northern ones do not contribute to reinstate you in America, who already enjoy the market for naval stores by the separation. You seem surprised that Holland does not pour in her succours, to maintain you mistress of the seas, when her own commerce is suffering by your act of navigation, or that any country should study her own interests while yours is on the carpet.

Such excesses of passionate folly, and unjust as well as unwise resentment, have driven you on, like Pharoah, to unpitied miseries, and while the importance of the quarrel shall perpetuate your disgrace, the flag of America will carry it round the world. The natural feelings of every rational being will take against you, and wherever the story shall be told, you will have neither excuse nor consolation left. With an unsparing hand and an unsatiable mind, you have havocked the world, both to gain dominion and to lose it, and while in a phrenzy of avarice and ambition, the east and the west are doomed to tributary bondage, you rapidly earned destruction as the wages of a nation. . . .

Number XIII

Philadelphia, April 19, 1783

"The times that tried mens souls," are over—and the greatest and completest revolution the world ever knew, gloriously and happily accomplished.

But to pass from the extremes of danger to safety— from the tumult of war, to the tranquility of peace, though sweet in contemplation, requires a gradual composure of the senses to receive it. Even calmness has the power of stunning, when it opens too instantly upon us. The long and raging hurricane that should cease in a moment, would leave us in a state rather of wonder than enjoyment; and some moments of recollection must pass, before we could be capable of tasting the full felicity of repose. There are but few instances, in which the mind is fitted for sudden transitions: It takes in its pleasures by reflection and comparison, and those must have time to act, before the relish for new scenes is complete.

In the present case—the mighty magnitude of the object—the various uncertainties of fate it has undergone—the numerous and complicated dangers we have suffered or escaped—the eminence we now stand on, and the vast prospect before us, must all conspire to impress us with contemplation.

To see it in our power to make a world happy—to teach mankind the art of being so—to exhibit on the theatre of the universe, a character hitherto unknown—and to have, as it were, a new creation entrusted to our hands, are honors that command reflection, and can neither be too highly estimated, nor too gratefully received.

In this pause then of recollection—while the storm is ceasing, and the long agitated mind vibrating to a rest, let us look back on the scenes we have passed, and learn from experience what is yet to be done.

Never, I say, had a country so many openings to happiness as this. Her setting out into life, like the rising of a fair morning, was unclouded and promising. Her cause was good. Her principles just and liberal. Her temper serene and firm. Her conduct regulated by the nicest steps, and every thing about her wore the mark of honor.

It is not every country (perhaps there is not another in the world) that can boast so fair an origin. Even the first settlement of America corresponds with the character of the revolution. Rome, once the proud mistress of the universe, was originally a band of ruffians. Plunder and rapine made her rich, and her oppression of millions made her great. But America needs never be ashamed to tell her birth, nor relate the stages by which she rose to empire.

The remembrance then of what is past, if it operates rightly, must inspire her with the most laudable of all ambition, that of adding to the fair fame she began with. The world has seen her great in adversity. Struggling without a thought of yielding beneath accumulated difficulties. Bravely, nay proudly, encountering distress, and rising in resolution as the storm encreased. All this is justly due to her, for her fortitude has merited the character. Let then the world see that she can bear prosperity: and that her honest virtue in time of peace, is equal to the bravest virtue in time of war.

She is now descending to the scenes of quiet and domestic life. Not beneath the cypress shade of disappointment, but to enjoy in her own land, and under her own vine, the sweet of her labors, and the reward of her toil—In this situation, may she never forget that a fair national reputation, is of as much importance as independence. That it possesses a charm which wins upon the world, and makes even enemies civil. That it gives a dignity which is often superior to power, and commands a reverence where pomp and splendor fail.

It would be a circumstance ever to be lamented and never to be forgotten, were a single blot, from any cause whatever, suffered to fall on a revolution, which to the end of time must be an honor to the age that accomplished it: and which has contributed more to enlighten the world, and diffuse a spirit of freedom and liberality among mankind, than any human event (if this may be called one) that ever preceded it.

It is not among the least of the calamities of a long continued war, that it unhinges the mind from those nice sensations which at other times appear so amiable. The continual spectacle of woe, blunts the finer feelings, and the necessity of bearing with the sight, renders it familiar. In like manner, are many of the moral obligations of society weakened, till the custom of acting by necessity, becomes an apology where it is truly a crime. Yet let but a nation conceive rightly of its character, and it will be chastly just in protecting it. None ever began with a fairer than America, and none can be under a greater obligation to preserve it.

The debt which America has contracted, compared with the cause she has gained, and the advantages to flow from it, ought scarcely to be mentioned. She has it in her choice to do, and to live, as happily, as she pleases. The world is in her hands. She has no foreign power to monopolize her commerce, perplex her legislation, or controul her prosperity. The struggle is over, which must one day have happened, and, perhaps, never could have happened at a better time.[1] And instead of a domineering

[1] That the revolution began at the exact period of time best fitted to the purpose, is sufficiently proved by the event—But the great hinge on which the whole machine turned is the UNION OF THE STATES: and this union was naturally produced by the inability of any one state to support itself against any foreign enemy without the assistance of the rest.

Had the states severally been less able than they were when the war began, their united strength would not have been equal to the undertaking, and they must, in all human probability, have failed—And on the other hand, had they severally been more able, they might not have seen, or, what is more, might not have felt the necessity of uniting; and either by at-

master, she has gained an *ally*, whose exemplary greatness, and universal liberality, have extorted a confession even from her enemies.

With the blessings of peace, independence, and an universal commerce, the states individually and collectively, will have leisure and opportunity to regulate and establish their domestic concerns, and to put it beyond the power of calumny to throw the least reflection on their honor. Character is much easier kept than recovered, and that man, if any such there be, who, from any sinister views, or littleness of soul, lends unseen his hand to injure it, contrives a wound it will never be in his power to heal.

As we have established an inheritance for posterity, let

tempting to stand alone, or in small confederacies, would have been separately conquered.

Now, as we cannot see a time (and many years must pass away before it can arrive) when the strength of any one state, or several united, can be equal to the whole of the present United States, and as we have seen the extreme difficulty of collectively prosecuting the war to a successful issue, and preserving our national importance in the world, therefore, from the experience we have had, and the knowledge we have gained, we must, unless we make a waste of wisdom, be strongly impressed with the advantage, as well as the necessity of strengthening that happy union which has been our salvation, and without which we should have been a ruined people.

that inheritance descend, with every mark of an honorable conveyance. The little it will cost, compared with the worth of the states, the greatness of the object, and the value of national character, will be a profitable exchange.

But that which must more forcibly strike a thoughtful penetrating mind, and which includes and renders easy all inferior concerns, is the UNION OF THE STATES. On this, our great national character depends. It is this which must give us importance abroad and security at home. It is through this only that we are, or can be nationally known in the world. It is the flag of the United States which renders our ships and commerce safe on the seas, or in a foreign port. Our Mediterranean passes must be obtained under the same stile. All our treaties whether of alliance, peace or commerce, are formed under the sovereignty of the United States, and Europe knows us by no other name or title.

The division of the empire into states is for our own convenience, but abroad this distinction ceases. The affairs of each state are local. They can go no farther than to itself. And were the whole worth of even the richest of them expended in revenue, it would not be sufficient to support sovereignty against a foreign attack. In short, we have no other national sovereignty than as United States. It would even be fatal for us if we had—too expensive to be maintained, and impossible to be supported. Individuals or individual states may call themselves what they please: but the world, and especially the world of enemies, is not to be held in awe by the whistling of a name. Sovereignty must have power to protect all the parts that compose and constitute it: and as UNITED STATES we are equal to the importance of the title, but otherwise we are not. Our union well and wisely regulated and cemented, is the cheapest way of being great—the easiest way of being powerful, and the happiest invention in government which the circumstances of America can admit of—Because it collects from each state, that which, by being inadequate, can be of no use to it, and forms an aggregate that serves for all.

The states of Holland are an unfortunate instance of the effects of individual sovereignty. Their disjointed condition exposes them to numerous intrigues, losses, calamities and enemies; and the almost impossibility of bringing their measures to a decision, and that decision into execution, is to them, and would be to us, a source of endless misfortune.

It is with confederated states as with individuals in society; something must be yielded up to make the whole secure. In this view of things we gain by what we give, and draw an annual interest greater than the capital.—I ever feel myself hurt when I hear the union, that great palladium of our liberty and safety, the least irreverently spoken of. It is the most sacred thing in the constitution of America, and that which every man should be most proud and tender of. Our citizenship in the United States is our national character. Our citizenship in any particular state is only our local distinction. By the latter we are known at home, by the former to the world. Our great title is, AMERICANS—our inferior one varies with the place.

So far as my endeavors could go, they have all been directed to conciliate the affections, unite the interests and draw and keep the mind of the country together; and the better to assist in this foundation-work of the revolution, I have avoided all the places of profit or office, either in the state I live in, or in the United States; kept myself at a distance from all parties and party connections, and even disregarded all private and inferior concerns: and when we take into view the great work we have gone through, and feel, as we ought to feel, the just importance of it, we shall then see, that the little wranglings and indecent contentions of personal parly, are as dishonorable to our characters, as they are injurious to our repose.

It was the cause of America that made me an author. The force with which it struck my mind, and the dangerous condition the country appeared to me in, by courting an impossible and an unnatural reconciliation with those who were determined to reduce her, instead of striking out into the only line that could cement and save her, A DECLARATION OF INDEPENDENCE, made it impossible for me, feeling as I did, to be silent: and if, in the course of more than seven years, I have rendered her any service, I have likewise added something to the reputation of literature, by freely and disinterestedly employing it in the great cause of mankind, and shewing there may be genius without prostitution.

Independence always appeared to me practicable and probable; provided the sentiment of the country could be formed and held to the object: and there is no instance in the world, where a people so extended, and wedded to former habits of thinking, and under such a variety of circumstances, were so instantly and effectually pervaded, by a turn in politics, as in the case of independence, and who supported their opinion, undiminished, through such a succession of good and ill fortune, till they crowned it with success.

But as the scenes of war are closed, and every man preparing for home and happier times, I therefore take my leave of the subject. I have most sincerely followed it from beginning to end, and through all its turns and windings: and whatever country I may hereafter be in, I shall always feel an honest pride at the part I have taken and acted, and a gratitude to Nature and Providence for putting it in my power to be of some use to mankind.